**For Erin**

There once was a girl with very long hair.

All the children laughed at her ...

And it made her despair.

She visited her good pal,
who made her feel better.

He said,
"Your hair is just fine, I wish it were mine."

There once was a boy,
who was very wide.

All the children laughed
at him ...

And so he cried.

He ran into his buddy, who made him feel good.

He said, "If I had your build, I would be thrilled!"

There once was a girl
with feet that were small.

All the children laughed
at her ...

And it made her bawl.

She visited her friend,
who dried up her tears.

He said,
"If I had your feet,
it would be neat!"

There once was a boy,
with very small ears.

All the children laughed at him ...

Which brought him
to tears.

He met his dear pal,
who had this to say:

"If I had your ears,
it would
make me cheer."

There once was a boy with very big eyes.

All the children laughed at him ...

Which caused him to cry.

He met his good friend and told her his problem.

She said, "Your eyes are just fine, you should not whine."

"How can you tell?
You cannot see."

"That's where you're wrong,
Now listen to me."

I see in
your heart,
and that's all
that counts.

Your inside is that to
which your true self amounts.

STRANGE  HAIRY  BALD  COOL  SMART  TALL  SMALL

WIDE  THIN  FUNNY  SERIOUS  SAD  HAPPY  FLUFFY

**All people are different on the outside, but equally special on the inside.**

13

If we all looked the same, it would be a shame.

We would not be able to tell one another apart.

# Never laugh at someone's outside, for it makes them feel blue.

## Treat people the way you would want them to treat you.

The children now learned the true meaning of beauty from the little blind girl, who taught them to see.

**Other cartoon books published by Gerard Arantowicz:**

**Penn State Life
Penn State Dance Marathon
Penn State Sports
Penn State Football
ABC's of Penn State**

**Write to P.O. Box 218
Baldwin City, KS 66006
to order**

# Differences

# Differences

Written and illustrated
by Gerard Arantowicz

Copyright 2002

Printed in the United States

ISBN: 1-58597-155-3

**LEATHERS**
PUBLISHING

A division of Squire Publishers, Inc.
4500 College Blvd.
Leawood, KS 66211
1/888/888-7696